Make Yourself Great Again!

PART I - THE REAL WORLD: HOW YOU'RE <u>TOLD</u> THINGS WORK

An Introduction to Mindset Stacking™ Solutions.

by **Dr. Robert C. Worstell**

Table of Contents

BONUS

Special Cheat Sheet Study Guide for This Part 1 is Ready For You To Download.

(for a limited time only)

Instant Access

Click or type into your browser:

http://livesensical.com/mygajoin/

INTRODUCTION

Have you ever had a complete melt-down, a real failure of your world-view, where the world has gone to hell and stayed there? Sad to tell you: *it's your own damned fault.*

What makes it worse is to find out that *everything you ever needed to succeed is already programmed into you* – and has been since you were born.

Then how did you get into that mess?

By believing what people told you as you were raised, and in every school you went to, all your on-the-job-training, all the books you ever read, every movie you ever saw, or song you ever heard. All those lessons and examples just helped you believe in something *other* than your own natural ability to succeed.

And so, if you were raised in a "disadvantaged" neighborhood, you weren't responsible for your own failures. However, this has only really been taught since just after World War II. Before that, there were many schools of thought which held that the individual created their own world and made their success in it, or didn't.

- W. Clement Stone believed in the Horatio Alger stories he read as a child and turned $100 into $35,000,000.

- George Washington Carver was born a slave and became one of the most respected and influential scientists of all time, even before the Civil Rights movement.

- Almost all of the U.S. Presidents were born into poor or decidedly middle-class backgrounds.

- Most of the Forbes list of Richest People came from a poor or middle-class upbringing and either didn't finish college or never went.

Some of our oldest traditions, such as the Tibetan Book of the Dead, say that as children we have complete access to all the world's knowledge – right up to the point we learn to talk. Yet other traditions say that everyone of us can *still* tap into unlimited knowledge, any time we want or need it.

Unfortunately, this isn't what modern Science says. And it isn't what any current government or their Academia wants you to believe.

The truth is wilder than our broadcast media admits, although our popular self-help and business books have published it every decade since books first came off a printing press (actually, even when they were still being hand-copied.)

That truth can be found in one of the oldest phrases, which has been repeated over and over in various ways through all our literature, philosophic, and religious works:

We Become What We Think About.

What you think and how you think is up to you. How you think consistently, the mental habits you've developed, are those you chose for yourself.

Those ideas you started relying on made you feel sexy, made you feel powerful, helped you think that others were looking up to you, and generally explained how the world worked. They gave you some prediction about things.

Then one day, your prediction failed you. What you used to think was the way the world worked, wasn't.

Yes, this happens several times to everyone. For a lot of people, this is also known as "mid-life crisis." But it can also happen in colleges with high-stress situations. The military sees people "hit the wall" in their boot camps weekly. Watch any popular movie and you'll see this happen to just about every single character. (Actually, we think it's a bad movie if that *doesn't* happen...)

We make our own movie called Life. We create our "real life" situations that we have to solve on our own. We each are the main hero or heroine, the director, and the producer. We stage each scene and sequence, we craft the dialog, we light the set, we pick the wardrobe, we provide the props, we edit out the bloopers. And our movie is a tragedy or comedy wholly dependent on the situations we find ourselves in. Life is a one-take continuing melodrama where there are no "do-overs."

Or so we think.

Is life really *that* serious?

Not if you know how it works, what the principles are behind the scenes, and how we each came to believe the specific world-view that we do. That we did. That we will tomorrow unless we decide to change it.

The movie each of us lives depends on the world view and mindset that we develop and stack as we live that movie. How we think creates that movie, determines if its a tragedy or comedy.

Perhaps the times where we are at our highest risk of having a tragic mental crash is in our current days when we are most removed from the natural world and have come to depend on all the concrete and steel environments where we live our lives.

These artificial worlds might protect us from the elements as long as we follow the rules they require. But they do not protect us if we build a world view which is fragile because it was built of straw instead of brick.

I've spent a few decades involved in the work of fixing people and thought I had it figured out, until my own world-view crashed. Then I spent another decade sorting out how that could have been possible at all.

This guide you are reading has a lot of my story, but it has more to the story of how the mental world we create really works.

It's been written for you to help you either recover from a recent crash, for help you make your belief-system more impervious to any future ones.

The third option is to help you *embrace* the crashes when they occur. That last one is for entrepreneurs, who take risks most of us wouldn't (but perhaps all of us should.)

You could say that crashes occur due to "brittle" world views. The belief-systems which are more resilient can withstand far more than we would ever ask of them.

If you want one of those resilient belief-systems, you're going to have to work out how to strip down and rebuild and tune your own mental engine *while* you are using it to drive to work every day *and* taking the kids to their sports events *or* visiting their relatives on the weekend. You can't just get away with putting it in the shop and driving a loaner.

You also meanwhile have to be prepared for environmental "crashes" and "adjustments."

- The economic crash of 2008 (like most recessions) affected a lot of people adversely. But a lot *more* people survived.

- The election of 2016 affected a lot of people adversely. But a lot _more_ people survived.

There will be more adverse situations/crashes/adjustments ahead. Because that's the cyclical history of this mud-ball we live on.

But believe it or not, it continues to get better.

Our beliefs themselves are what get us into trouble.

RETURN TO THE BEGINNING AND START FROM THERE

There I was, just starting the first leg of a 1700-mile road trip near twilight, heading away from the sunset into darkness. This wasn't my ideal time to start rebuilding my life. But it was the cards I'd been dealt.

I had all my belongings packed into the back of a smallish rental truck. This was all that I had left or considered actually valuable from 20-plus year career of working for a syndicated self-help cult.

After all that time, their promises and ideals quit ringing true. They were as hollow as the Academy award statues that were set up every year just down the street in Hollywood. Or the tinsel signage that announced Christmas was here, in a town that probably never ever saw snow (except on distant mountains.)

It seemed ironic that the "International Management Headquarters" for this corporation was smack-dab downtown in a city that was built on the premise of inventing fiction, projecting their stories on huge screens while people sat in the dark, gorging themselves on popcorn, carbonated soft drinks, and sticky-sugary treats.

Why I had left was a good question.

It was a failure, both mine and the syndicate. It had finally become clear that this Syndicate was only there to make a rich lifestyle for the Founder and top execs. But that was never obvious to those of us who had invested our lives in forwarding their dogmas. "Save the Planet" was the mantra, and the unspoken subtitle caption was "as long as our Founder gets rich."

(While you probably have guessed the name of this cult, we don't need to go there, as the name itself leaves a taint wherever it's used. And this book is here to help you, not upset you.)

Once that Founder died, the internal wars quickly started and quickly ended as one person forcibly assumed the mantle. Within a few years, you saw only his image on the screen at events we all had to attend. This new CEO was the new face of their Syndicate. But the "Old Man" was gone, and with him went most of the human PR touch that kept their system alive all those years.

What the new leader brought was fear, which soon translated down through the management ranks to everyone else.

Cut the core out of an apple and it starts rotting from the inside, while the outside still stays shiny. For awhile, at least.

I'd been in touch with the CEO and his top "lieutenants" on things that didn't seem to be working like they used to. Unfortunately, what I got back as answers just confirmed the problem. Fear was now King. Policy was Dead.

Once that scene became obvious to me, I had to leave. This explained why it was getting harder to get things done, why more non-sense was being used to keep things patched together. The staff were operating more and more on fear. It had become impossible to fix anything, let alone understand them. All my efforts to understand were running into more and more roadblocks built of non-sensical explanations.

If I stayed, I'd have to accept a mindset as crazy as the world around it.

So I got a rental truck and started driving. Out onto unknown roads with only a road map to guide me. Darkness ahead, and darkness behind. But there was also a sense of freedom in this journey. An understanding that as the world turned, there was inevitable sunshine ahead.

It would be days before I reached my Midwestern destination. Plenty of time to think things through as I drove.

IS THIS STORY YOURS?

Do you see yourself here?

What a person believes is important.

So is selecting the foundation for a house you're building.

Just as you don't build your own house on rented land, or sand, your own internal world can be accidentally built based on ideas which you haven't examined.

I had been through 20 years of believing certain "facts" to be true, when they were actually just made up. But the beliefs were so strong, that the arguments (also based on those "facts") were held in place despite contradictions obvious on all sides.

All those facts turned out to be sand, taken from earlier authors in snippets, without attribution. Not even rented, but lifted wholesale. So the original rock-solid ideas were ground to pebbles, then sand, and only then held together like a sand sculpture with water. That works until the strong sunshine of workable truths start drying things out.

This is what cults do. They re-interpret other data in light of their own pre-set "facts" so that everything still aligns.

The end of a cult is when the personal benefits of following are outweighed by penalties for continuing. Individuals start realizing that the world outside doesn't follow those "facts" they'd swallowed.

This is known as a paradigm shift. It's also known as a belief crisis. A mental crash.

When cults have too many people seeing through their "facts," they collapse.

Another word for this is Failure.

Entrepreneurs have said often that the road to success is paved with failure. Edison himself said that he needed to make 10,000 failures in order to make the one success of the electric light bulb. WD40, the remarkable loosener for stuck bolts and nuts, was reportedly preceded by 39 earlier attempts.

But people don't often view their on lives as a Startup.

Perhaps they should.

Might be less painful.

What do you think?

THERE ARE NO RIGHT OR WRONG BELIEFS, JUST SOME THAT WORK.

We can fall on both sides of this issue. And that point is exactly where this book and its research initially started.

It's too easy to consider that "only fanatics have weird beliefs." And that miracles are somehow unobtainable by the ordinary person on the street.

The truth to these two statements may be shocking.

Beliefs become "weird" when the environment outside doesn't match up with their "facts." This is evident where the bi-coastal blue state residents don't understand the flyover red state residents and vice-versa.

Meanwhile, we daily perform what would seem "miracles" just a few decades ago, because we believe in the technology we use. Cell phones were the stuff of Star Trek in the late '60's. We have the Apple watch today, but the first Dick Tracy 2-way radio appeared by cartoon in 1952. Meanwhile, we are in the era of self-driving cars and on the verge of seeing flying ones.

For now, just take these ideas and plant them on your mental back-burner for consideration.

Your mind is filled with beliefs. You believe all sorts of things, not just your political or religious (or even sexual) preferences. Anything that ever makes it into the broadcast news is based on someone's belief they want you to share.

As a test, sit down with a notepad one night in front of the TV (as long as you can stand it) and study what passes for news, or even entertainment. Start noting down the beliefs they assume you have as well as the ones they are pushing on you now.

It starts with the idea that the persons behind the TV images you see actually exist somewhere, that the events they are talking about actually occurred the way they are telling you.

In between, you can study the advertisements, which are telling you what they believe about you and what your needs and wants are, and how much you are willing to buy something to get them.

Their beliefs. Your beliefs.

And your beliefs create your success or lack of it.

This book is to lay out the ground rules so that you can start improving your own progress toward those needs and wants you've been seeking.

The basic: *Beliefs aren't permanent.* They change all the time. Their only power is the faith you put behind them. And you can and do change them anytime you feel like it.

Everything on this planet runs on beliefs.

It can be said that the world around us is that way because we believed it into existence and continue to believe it that that way.

It is, then: change your beliefs, change your world.

If that's really what you want out of life, anyway.

THE PEACE THAT STARTED A MENTAL WAR

The beginning of the end started over a year before I left.

The Founder had already been gone for a few years, and the new CEO was slowly increasing his control through management lines below him. Long-serving executives got moved around, demoted. Policies got "corrected." And generally, things were making less and less sense.

I'd moved off internal correction (fixing people by talking to them and helping them apply the relevant policy to their situation) as it wasn't working any more. I could only "fix" people for shorter and shorter periods of time before they wound up before me again as "broke" (or were moved to another job entirely.)

As we were allowed some time off every year, I tried to visit family on those occasions, to the farm I grew up on.

One nice vacation day in summer, humid and hot, the two family dogs and I were out for a walk. Pausing in the shade of a several-hundred-year-old massive oak, it hit me.

All mental noise dropped away.

I was left with a feeling of peace, quiet, sublime calm.

The birds were singing, the wind wafting through the leaves and branches.

Everything else was gone.

Quiet.

I was at peace. And I didn't know how I had gotten there.

But I enjoyed it thoroughly while it lasted. I don't know how long it lasted as time seemed to stand still.

At last, the first thought that came was: "What is this, how did it happen, and how can I make it happen again?"

But there was no answer.

So I looked over what I had done that day, what I had eaten, how I had slept.

Still no answer.

Yet I recognized that this was a high personal state that the Syndicate's teachings didn't cover. This was what they should be helping people achieve, but instead had them on a constantly shifting route which lead them all onto their next paid service.

Obviously, once you achieved this, you wouldn't need anything the Syndicate was offering after that. Provided you could re-experience it at will.

Later that day, and days after that, I found that I could re-enter that state and not have to be near that particular tree at all.

When I returned to L.A. I brought that peace with me. Standing in a 6th floor room overlooking the noisy, crowded, air-polluted city: it was there again. And I could mostly keep it going for as long as I wanted.

Nothing in what I had been taught, nothing of what I had studied, nothing in all that I had used to help "fix" people - none of these were actually designed to achieve this state.

And yet, there I was, able to re-experience this rare state at will. This ability had nothing to do with all I had been through in that Syndicate. That peace wasn't trained in, or enabled through their expensive counseling.

Peace was the tipping point.

I'd already been reviewing and re-studying the Syndicate policy, all the data I had trained on and used. I was testing all of this to work out if and why it needed fixing. All that data was supposed to be perfect, but the more I looked, the more it turned out flawed.

Finding that tipping point took me over the edge.

It took me another year to get myself extracted according to their rules. That itself was a test of their policies. And it turned out that no one there could do a damned thing about my situation. I had fallen into a very wide crack in their foundation which no one had a solution for.

Yes, there were solutions in that policy, but they weren't being applied.

Because people were afraid. Fear was motivating people more far than their expressed-as-policy purpose of helping others improve themselves. They couldn't help because they were afraid for their own positions in the Syndicate.

I wasn't afraid of anything. I had found peace.

I still didn't understand how I had gotten to this state, or how to help anyone else achieve it. I did understand that staying there was interfering with my own research into resolving those two questions.

So I planned, and left.

THE SAME IS ALWAYS DIFFERENT, SOMEHOW

You don't just show up somewhere after 20 years and expect everything to be the same.

Time does that.

Sure, the fences were still there. They had a few more patches, but were in the same place.

The barn was there, but my Dad had added onto it with an extension.

The original house was there. It was leaning a little more, and some of the living room floor was a bit more "bouncy". But that hundred-year-old house still had a few more years in it.

The people were 20 years older. And they had changed a bit in their attitudes.

But still, honestly happy to see me.

I had changed.

And I'd come back with questions. Lots of questions.

Because my own world had just fallen apart.

I came back much as I had left. Little money in the bank, but with credit card debt that needed to be paid. No job. No vehicle. A few clothes. Lots of books.

Then, as now, willing to work.

So it took a few months to get to a place where those questions could start to be answered. I had to get a job. I borrowed my parent's truck to get to work until one day my brother showed up with one I could buy from him.

The job was entry-level warehouse work. I got trained on running a forklift and how to manage their paperwork. And did OK in general.

This also enabled me to get a regular Internet connection.

So my research continued. Anytime I wasn't working, I was online, looking up stuff.

Now I was able to start.

WHAT IS THE "REAL WORLD"?

I was supposed to be happy to return to the real world, even if I was in debt, no pension, no certificates or diplomas worth anything. That's the conventional wisdom when someone frees themselves from a cult.

But after awhile, I began to have my doubts again.

People often refer to the "real" world as if it's a natural thing - it's not.

Our humankind existence is very much culture-driven. And that culture is based on a lot of assumptions which are usually untested and mostly untrue.

These assumptions are given by the authorities. But who says they were tested and true to begin with? Authorities have to be trusted to be believed.

Let's go into what makes an authority in our culture:

1. It has to be Science-based to be believable.

Meaning, if someone did a study on it, then it's got to be true.

The problem with this is that almost all scientific studies are at least half-wrong. (See Appendix for the scientific study that "proved" it.)

When one of their studies exposes the idea that "all scientific studies are at least half-wrong" then we have to consider perhaps that Science doesn't always know best.

(And a "banned" TED talk speaks to this – see Appendix.)

2. You can believe your Government.

Both Pew and Gallup say different - that less than half of the people believe the government will do something right or even tell the truth. This has been consistent opinion for decades, enough to raise a new generation or two. (In Appendix.)

3. You can trust the Mainstream News to be accurate and honest.

Well, no. See Associated Press article (in Appendix.) You might figure that broad Internet access has had something to do with this.

4. And then there is the unsung villain to all this, Conventional Wisdom.

Wiktionary has this defined as:

> n. A belief or set of beliefs that is widely accepted, especially one which may be questionable on close examination.

The problem is that when looking up quotes on Conventional Wisdom, you'll find that it's considered to be mostly wrong, and going the opposite way is more profitable.

Such as:

> The only way to get ahead is to find errors in conventional wisdom.
> Larry Ellison

> To build a great company, which is a CEO's job, sometimes you have to stand up against conventional wisdom.
> Carly Fiorina

*Conventional wisdom is no wisdom at all.
Conventional wisdom is taking somebody else's
word for the way things are. It's the followers of
this world who rely on assumption. Not the leaders.*
Richard Marcinko

*Whenever you find yourself on the side of the
majority, it's time to reform.*
Will Rogers

The trick to this is that for most people, it's easily accepted and seldom examined.

The obvious survival reaction is being instantly highly skeptical about anything and everything you run hear, read, or view if

      a) It's backed by Science,

      b) It's stated by anyone in government,

      c) You heard it on the news, or

      d) one of your friends says it in passing as if it's the latest version of Gospel.

Now lets take this backwards.

Who educated you? Was it a government-sponsored school?

Were you enabled to run experiments in class (like Chemistry) to prove for yourself that datum was correct?

Which of the various textbooks you read actually proved their statements as accurate - particularly history or current events? Just because a lot of people say the same thing doesn't mean that it happened that way or that it happened at all.

Did the author only reference a single scientific study or magazine article as a link?

Obviously, you should be testing all your material to see if it "makes sense."

But who ever defined what that phrase means?

I did find one finally, after a half-century of batting off stuff I was told or ran into which didn't make sense to me - but I couldn't say why.

When I studied Marketing, one datum stood out and addressed this: people decide emotionally and justify logically. Benefits sell and features seal the deal.

People act to buy something when it makes sense to them. It resonates with them emotionally and also rationally. And then they pay for it or charge it, and take it home (or download it.) Free might not be a real exception. How much of the free stuff you downloaded did you actually open and read or put to use? Most of us have tons of stuff on our hard-drive that we paid only an email address for. But it was sensible enough at the time, particularly for that price or that guarantee.

What makes sense to one person won't make sense to another. Because we are individuals and have to stack our mindset to fit our own particular requirements. Even identical twins won't share the same mindset.

All that is asked here is that you take over how your mindset is being stacked.

Back to assumptions. Our world is full of them. And this is what is called, the "real" world. This is the one that is supposed to make the worlds of fantasy and imagination pale by comparison.

But practically, this "real world" is full of fantasy reasoning and imagined events.

People believe what they want, and this creates the world they live in.

This is the world we grew up in. This is the world we see around us now.

This is the "real world" I returned to after living in the Syndicate's custom version of it for over 20 years.

I'm not saying that you can't trust authorities, I'm just saying that you need to test everything you encounter.

Disagree?

Well, have you tested *everything* you've read, heard, or been taught? Come back when you have and we'll discuss it...

(I've included a short discussion about this chapter in the Appendix in the Notes section.)

WHAT MAKES AN AUTHORITY?

People follow an insane amount of other people these days, most they've never met in person. They accept what these strangers say almost without question. What these people recommend and state as bald fact is swallowed whole.

These are the "influencers" that marketing types constantly seek out in order to have a "popular" or "viral" hit on their hands. Get one of these guys to recommend your product and the sales take off.

Politicians surround themselves with these types in order to get elected. They are called "celebrities". Scientists contact these types in order to get funding for their research.

The writer is told to go off and get a "platform", and only then come back with their book proposal. What they mean by a platform is a set of followers who accept your message routinely and will buy something if you recommend it.

How do these influencers get such followings?

They routinely give useful data, stuff that helps people. In marketing-speak, it's data that is one of three classes: entertaining, educational, or inspirational (enlightening.)

Why are these three classes sought after?

People want to have more feelings in their lives.

Entertainment can give you a wide variety of stimulation that can bring about all manner of emotional states and feelings. Learning something new is always a feel-good scene, if you're successful (even if it's how to avoid disaster.) Being inspired is a short cut to feeling hope in your life again, especially as our culture seems to be filled with hope-destroying news and marketing these days. Life itself can hand you bitter disappointments routinely - unless you make it a habit to find what is good around you.

People become authorities by helping you feel good about yourself, or at least giving you a welcome distraction and emotional release.

And this is why actors and actresses are able to hire themselves out as product pitch-persons. People liked their performances as they make them feel better, so marketers find that such followers will also buy something if a celebrity comes out and recommends a brand (like that of a certain politician.) That celebrity could be clueless about the politician's actual intentions or voting record. Celebrities are people and themselves could simply be following some other follower – and getting paid for it.

When authorities routinely give you material that's useful, then you start tuning into what they say as a habit.

The warning is not to follow someone blindly. Most of our fast food and our entertainment is built on this addictive "instant gratification." Fast food is designed to be filling and is laced with ingredients that makes your glands secrete just like when you feel good. Sugar, fried foods, salt – eating these things all give you a "zing!" Entertainment is designed with visuals and music that gets your heart-beat moving faster. And a good story will resonate in your body itself, stimulating feelings as you read (see Chris Vogler's *Writer's Journey* for a chapter on how this works.)

Look over your own influencers. Check out what you are eating - is it addictive? Look at what you really like to read or watch - is it filled with emotional roller-coaster rides and cliff-hanging suspense? Study the people who write stuff you always open and read - are they routinely giving you valuable data you can use to become more efficient or prosperous?

Value.

Real authorities constantly add value to your life.

Fake authorities don't.

If you study what data-sources you have in your life, you'll also find people you quit listening to. Study these over as well and you'll see the patterns show up about how they gave you bad data in the past.

More often than not, you'll find a lot of *following-followers*. They are following those who they think are "thought leaders" or "influencers." They are wannabe authorities and are just parroting what others say and do. They add no real value.

Another type you'll find is *short-cutters*. People who are constantly giving you data so you can "get rich quick" or some other "fast" method that only works for a very short time.

Classic texts are classic because they tell you the natural laws at work. They are also entertaining, educational, and inspirational. Often all at the same time. They may mention other authors, but they are unique in their approach, not copycat. Because of this, you can read and re-read these books and even recorded music or videos, and get more out of what they tell you every time. Every single time.

Real leaders have a consistency about them which doesn't change whether people follow them or not. It's called integrity. This makes them easy to follow, but harder to emulate.

Those are the real authorities.

Most of our popular culture is like a swarm of jelly fish. They do move, but in groups, and often with the tides that surround them. Cattle move somewhat like this as well.

They like to stay in herds for various reasons. Humankind is yet another herd animal.

Wannabe authorities are trying to take advantage of this. Unfortunately, they are short-cutters and are really just following-followers. They try to see where the crowd is heading and then get in front of it as an early adopter, so they look like a leader.

You can find them as they are constantly shifting their approach and what they are pushing. They take every short cut imaginable to get out in front fastest.

I keep a few of these appearing in my inbox just so I can see by their email headings where they think their mob is going next (the next "big" thing). This tells me where not to go, as this is a pure example of conventional wisdom. (This is where I love Gmail because it separates the chaff from the wheat for me. If I keep getting inane offers from someone instead of real value, they go into "promotion" category, where I can bulk select and delete without opening.)

There is a short-cut technique that the bulk of marketers seem to use these days, based on psycho-babble. These guys say and repeat the idea that people are motivated by either "fear" or "greed." And there is just enough truth in that so they can keep making money off their sales pitches. But the main desires and their derivatives are much broader than that. When you see this technique (and it seems that the "news" sites and networks are 95% devoted to pitches like these – Fox News and Drudge are no better than MSNBC, CNN, or Huffington Post) then you know there isn't all that much value in these areas.

It's time to look through your authorities with a keen eye for these factors: short-cutting, following-followers, and real value-adders. Quit listening to the first two and concentrate on the last one for awhile. Then see if you don't start feeling better about life.

There is an observation that the terrorist organizations around us are existing mostly because of the "news" they get. Internally, they are self-destructive. Pushing fear all the time tends to create more fear.

Frankly, our news organizations are using a mild form of terrorism themselves. The only way you'll reform them is to quit watching and listening.

Subscribe only to sites which add value to your life.

Find real authorities and follow those.

And you'll feel better routinely.

INTERMISSION

All of this can be heavy going. It's a lot to take in at one time.

If this were a ball game, we'd have a half-time right here. Time for taking a break, hitting the refrigerator, and so on.

Instead of commercials, matching bands, and grinning cheerleaders, we'll instead give you our own offer.

1. A Cheat Sheet

Specifically designed to get you through all this thick training by selecting just the key points to test for yourself.

It's in PDF format and quite easy to understand. Just a few pages, actually.

2. Cutting Room Floor Chapters

This book got too thick, so I thinned it down just to the data you really needed to know. Not that the rest of it wasn't valuable.

But really, you have the rest of your life to soak this in and re-stack your mindset. The best advice for this book is to give it a break for a few days and then start over from the beginning and really test what you study.

To help you distract yourself for those few days, I've got all these chapters set up in PDF format so you can download and study them, put them on your smartphone or tablet, and review them whenever and wherever you want.

3. Special Discounts on Other Versions

I've got a line with the publisher to give you the print versions for 50% off. I'm also looking around to what I can do with the audio versions.

So I want to pass these on to you as well.

4. Upcoming Online Courses

While this offer already has an email course as part of it, I've also got a full video course in the works which will take all of this and cut it into easier parts to study and understand.

As I've said, this is an introduction to learning how to re-stack your own mindset the way you want it. So it's key for you to be able to really know all the steps you need to take to Make Yourself Great Again.

What's It Going to Cost?

Only your email.

And I won't nag you about things or give you useless offers.

I also don't give anyone else access to my lists. Because you wouldn't want me to treat you that way.

Just go to this link and click on it:

http://livesensical.com/mygajoin/

PS. There are a lot more discoveries I'll keep you up to date on. And you can email me directly after that, as well. We can have all the discussions you want. Your choice.

See you on the inside.

And now, back to the game in progress...

JUST GO TH*NK YOURSELF.

The problem with self help is that it's just too personal.

For 20 years I'd been working 60- and 70-hour weeks for a Syndicate, dedicated to the idea of just giving everything I had to help people improve their lives.

And nothing to show for it.

Just memories.

Now I had a job and started to have some spare time where questions could creep in that needed answers.

Why had I been there and done all that? Was it just a joke? A scam? Does Self-Help actually work - or is it just a bunch of scammers?

That last was the core question which haunted me.

The short answer turned out: no. Self-Help does work where it's actually based on natural principles. And those principles haven't changed since before humankind started recording our history.

With an Internet connection, you can find out just about anything about anything. The world is at your fingertips. And all the worlds which had ever been.

So I started my studies.

It turned out that where a person gets a result in self-help, the latest book or program or course might get the praise, but that's not necessarily what caused the improvement. There are thousands of factors which could be given as why the improvement happened. Similarly, any failure may or may not be what that person last used as a product, so blaming them may or may not be accurate.

That doesn't even cover the idea of a placebo (sugar pills.) This is where the person's expectations produce the actual result.

But the bulk of the scams in Self-Help observably come from over-charismatic types who are pitching a short-cut method.

You can probably think of a few you've heard of or even experienced. This is why they had to invent the FTC. Just to get ride herd on snake-oil and Used Car salespeople. (I'm not saying the FTC is effective, just why they were invented.)

Diet plans are like this. Some even have been accused of killing people.

Cults are associated with Kool-Aid drinking thanks to Jim Jones and his Guyana cult who killed themselves with poison-laced Kool-Aid on their way to "salvation."

This brings us right back to over-charismatic types running things.

The Syndicate was built from it's Founder's early work in establishing franchises all over the U.S. and some foreign countries. All based on his personal charisma, and using that to get people to follow him and his practices.

That was the first stumbling block in these studies. Personal charisma needed to be eliminated.

So the first test was, did any self-help author's books still sell well even after the author.s death?

Books would insulate you from the various persuasive arts of the spoken word and video tricks.

Going through Gutenberg.org and other online public domain sites, I was able to find many self-help books that were being downloaded regularly. Since most of these were pre-1923, it was pretty certain that their author had passed on.

Taking the top books which were downloaded regularly also found them being sold online, which is the point of bestsellers with (long) dead authors.

So the charisma factor could be ruled out, as well as some Syndicate or other organization selling books on that person's behalf.

Next was to read these books and see what key points they pushed and which of these were held in common with at least one other book on that list.

A grid was made up of the common factors. I had a dozen books and drew the line at having common factors present in at least a third of them. (See my *Go Thunk Yourself* for the grid and full study – follow the link to my book site in Appendix.)

This then gave me 14 elements that might point to a natural system of self-help.

And they did.

There are tools now which make a cross-comparative study easier. (Meaning, you can check my work.)

Comparing these 14 elements to the Syndicate practices found that they were using only short-cut alterations of these natural principles.

The burning question was then: why weren't the Syndicate's short cuts obvious, and why did I have to leave and find out this research on my own?

Because the Founder (and later, that new CEO) added complexity and claimed they had discovered or invented them personally.

Businesses keep making money off their followers by delivering something new to them. "If you liked that, then you're going to love this..."

You saw that in the "Internet Marketers" described above. Keep Inventing and Selling Something is their model. (Oh, you thought KISS meant "keep it simple, scholar?")

And there's that Peace point I was telling you about... Just research through old philosophy and religious texts and you'll find that that peace state is one of the highest ones they attained.

The trick in cults and marketing scams is to give them yet another reason to keep coming back after you've achieved that for them.

In Religions (Capital "R") you'll find that it's gotten very, very complex. And few, if any of their followers are even awarded sainthood.

The more complex the system, the easier it is to fail. This is a rule of engineering - the more moving parts, the easier it is to have something break.

But in the most complex systems, it's often hard to find what broke first. The complexity will tend to also support minor failures for a long time.

In short, the Syndicate teachings quit working. Not just because their new CEO was wrecking their management. He and his cronies had also been fiddling with the Founder's materials to make them even more complex. But the Founder himself had already "complexified" his own teachings beyond simple workability. And that is why they had to send people to "Advanced" franchises in the Syndicate to get the "best" results (also, the most expensive.)

Nature works all the time. So when you isolate the natural principles at work, it's dead simple, isn't it?

Well, yes and no.

Our society has now gotten so complex that we are living very un-natural lives. Our lifestyles are complex beyond belief. (How many electronic devices do you have in your life daily - and which of these could you fix or get fixed easily?)

Meanwhile, the original teachings which long ago told us simply how to attain these high personal states have been "translated" and "interpreted" to a point where you can't even study the original works and make any sense out of them, much less attain any expected results that are claimed.

For instance, the New Testament books were all written long after the death of Jesus, based on stories passed down for generations. And there are really just four or six versions of his teachings. These are called the Gospels. The rest of the books in that collection were written by church administrators.

If you just read the "items in red" (what Jesus is actually reputed to have said) then you see an incredibly powerful set of stories which have come down through the ages. But the text of those words fit into a book which is barely long enough to be printed. (I did this once - two versions together came out to about 45 pages of text.)

The point of all of this was to find out if there was a way people could improve themselves regardless of charismatic leaders.

And it's true. We can and do change ourselves.

Later studies showed that this is native, we were born with it, and we do it every day and moment of our lives. On a longer scale, it's called evolution. On a monthly basis, it's known as habit stacking. On a day-to-day basis, it's called stacking your mindset.

HOW TO FIGURE THINGS OUT AND TEST THEM FOR YOURSELF

While I was sorting out Self-Help, a funny thing happened. I wasn't sure I knew how to investigate and analyze anything.

So I had to pause that study, step back, and study how to study. I had to analyze analysis. All without any proven study or analysis tools.

Tricky.

But it was again that start-up approach. Work in iterations. Added to that was the pragmatic farmer/engineer upbringing: to use the tools you have to get the job done and meanwhile, create the tools you need to do a better job.

Above, you heard about natural systems. When I was growing up, some of the big, popular books were Rachel Carson's "Silent Spring" and Paul Erlich's "Population Bomb." These books made some very important points. However, history wasn't kind to them.

- Far from being permanent, removing DDT from sprays proved that it didn't have any continuing or residual effect on our bird populations. (Unfortunately, for certain countries, it also brought back Malaria as they now had nothing as effective to kill mosquitoes.)

- As nations improve their disposable income, by building their middle class, the numbers of children per family drop. And now several nations have negative population growth. As immigrants entered these countries, they also raised their own standards of living and also quit having as many children.

- Natural systems are also playing havoc with other popular books. Everyone agrees that the climate changes, but it's a 50/50 split on exactly how it's changing. (Which is why the term "Global Warming" was turned into "Climate Change.")

Nature has a habit of healing itself, as long as it's not interfered with too much. Humankind has made more than one desert. But, if they emulate Nature and replant according to Nature's rules, they are able to regenerate the land. Unfortunately, this isn't widely known. You can see areas which were part of the great Dust Bowl of the '30's which are being farmed today and not eroding even in a drought. Farmers changed their practices. They started farming like Nature does - different plants every year, and a diverse variety of them. And it turned out some of that land should only be grazed, or managed for sustainable forestry.

Natural systems also apply to analysis. The Scientific Method has been widely used, as it's really based on observing how successful people work things out.

Despite how the Academia have turned it into complicated processes with twenty-some steps and verified only by advanced calculus, it can be quite simple. (You just have to take it back to the version the Ancient Greeks used.)

But it also isn't a simple, one-time sequence. It's a system. Once you improve something, you can turn around and continue to improve it.

Here's the short-hand:

1. Look over something.

2. Get an idea of how it could be improved, get a plan.

3. Execute that plan and see the results.

4. Finally, compare those results back against what the scene is now.

1-2-3-4, rinse, repeat.

That's a four point analysis system. It's natural, as you'll see anything living on this planet uses this. Nature is abundant and pervasive because it uses systems like this.

This system can also test anything you are told, read, or view.

1. Start out with what results you want.

2. Then observe what's there and work out what should be changed to achieve those results - which gives you a plan.

3. Execute that plan.

4. Are those results then closer or further from what you want or need?

Someone gives you a datum. If you try to apply this datum, does it give you the expected result? Look closely, and you'll see those four points there again. That datum should give you expected results. If it doesn't then the datum as given doesn't work. You can run it through a few more times, if you can figure that maybe you need to tweak this or that - but if it keeps coming up with different results than you expect, it's a false datum.

So now I had an analysis system.

Applying this to self help, the idea came: if self-help is based on a natural system it would be successful in its results.

OK, I can hear you from here. And the warning is this: *look out for short cuts.*

Monsanto tried this with their Roundup Ready herbicide and genetically-modified plants. About the time their patent ran out, Nature had already started producing Roundupresistant weeds. And a decade after that patent expiration, people are moving off Roundup and glysophate-based herbicides as they don't work as promised any more. They are moving to alternating herbicides and pesticides, as well as changing their tillage and planting habits.

In short, they've gone to what worked before this "breakthrough." Monsanto had a great run, made a lot of money, sued a lot of farmers for mis-using their patented seeds. A quarter-century later, it didn't matter. (And we're side-stepping what genetically-modified plants and glysophate may or may not do to animal and human consumers.)

"Internet Marketers" also have this problem: there are a certain crowd who have attracted a following of gullible consumers who will buy the "latest thing" in online marketing. The problem is that by the time these guys write up and package what quickly made them millions, is that they no longer work.

When you really look at what they were doing, it was to use shady Internet Marketing tactics to sell Internet Marketing packages to Internet Marketing wannabes. Since their sales "proved" those packages worked, it was a continuing vicious cycle.

(Why it actually continues to work is that most people who buy courses never complete them. The whole system runs on charisma. See something familiar here?)

And these Internet Marketers shared their lists with their network by promoting those other people's products to their lists. Meanwhile, they cross-coordinated their releases so that they weren't stepping on each other's toes. This means that most of the people they email to are on several of their fellow Internet Marketer's lists as well. And this group of people is happy to buy their stuff and put the package on their living room shelves as a trophy.

These Internet Marketers know people probably won't get through the course they offer before they get the next offer to buy. And the entertainment value of their pitches keeps those customers in a buying mood. So they pitch the next guy's stuff and rake in commissions for those sales. And so it continues, round-robin. Meanwhile, their buying public keep their Day Jobs, for sure.

Are these Internet Marketers doing anything to improve humanity? Only to the degree they keep cheering people up.

Did Monsanto help? For awhile. Now, not so much.

But at last I had a way to study broad classes of things to find the natural systems which made them work.

And now, you do too.

CHARACTERS YOU SHOULD MEET (IF YOU HAVEN'T ALREADY.)

My best friends seem to be authors I've never met in person. Many were dead before I was born.

You've probably run into this. You're reading along and this guy or gal seems to be reading your mind as you read their books. What they are saying has so much truth in it, and must have been written just for you.

Here's the key authors who have turned out to be my main mentors on this journey:

1. **Earl Nightingale** – As a Marine on board the Arizona during the Japanese attack on Pearl Harbor, he was blown overboard unconscious by an explosion. Another naval officer assisted him to shore. Yet he's never told this story himself in all the thousands of recordings he made for "Our Changing World" or any of the lectures he recorded for Nightingale-Conant.

Instead, he talked often of his upbringing during the Depression, where his family found themselves in a Tent City in Long Beach after their father had left. His fascination at age 12 was why some people were rich and others poor – what was the key to success?

His mother's love of books and reading inspired him to find the Long Beach library and become an avid reader. For the rest of his life, he followed this quest to discover the secret of success.

The result was becoming the top radio announcer in the biggest radio corporation in Chicago. Yet he left that job only two years later, when he had several businesses going. One, an insurance company, was used to his weekly pep talks and asked him to record a version to play while he was gone on a planned vacation.

His Gold recording The Strangest Secret resulted, and started a new industry of self-improvement recordings.

His real success started skyrocketing when he read a book by...

2. **Napoleon Hill** – If not for his stepmother, Hill might have had a disastrous end. Born in the poor hills of Wise County, Virginia, by age nine he had taken to carrying a six-shooter in his belt and was aiming to follow the footsteps of his hero, Jesse James. His stepmother came into his life, saw the grief in his future, and so changed the course of the whole family.

For Napoleon, at age twelve she got him to trade in his six-gun for a typewriter, with the idea he could gain fame and fortune more than any outlaw. Hill was an avid reader by that time and saw the result in books that could spread a person's ideas far beyond a single village in the backwoods. By 14 he was writing freelance for a local paper who needed news stories.

His key incident was meeting Andrew Carnegie in 1908, there to get a story about inspiring people of his day. 3 days later, as Hill reports in his books, he was commissioned perform what became a life-long mission – to assemble and distill the Philosophy of Achievement. The rags to riches story of Carnegie matched his own start in Virginia coal country. He had the tools he needed, the skills and experience to get started.

And he wound up making more people rich than Carnegie had.

It is no wonder that most successful people you know have read and studied his book, deeply influenced in their own success.

3. **Dorothea Brande** – She was known as a top-flight editor and writer. But it wasn't always that way. In her own terms, she was a failure. Educated at the University of Chicago and Michigan, she was employed as an associate editor for the American Review.

She hit upon a remarkable idea one day when reading a psychology text that changed her life forever. As she details it, before that point she was completing less than two works a year outside of her work. In the two years after this discovery, she had written "Three books (the first two in just two weeks less than the first year, and both successful in their different fields), twenty-four articles, four short stories, seventy-two lectures, the scaffolding of three more books; and innumerable letters of consultation and professional advice sent to all parts of the country."

Her discovery gave the mantra: "Act as if it were impossible to fail."

This simple belief, put into action, seems to dissolve the dam of willful failure and let loose a flood of ability.

4. **Claude M. Bristol** – Little is known of Bristol's early life outside of what he discussed in his books. When sent overseas during WWI, he arrived before his papers and so could not be paid. While he was fed and housed as good as any of the other enlisted men, it rubbed him raw that others could buy chewing gum or have a smoke when he couldn't. So he made up his mind never to be without money again after he left the service.

While he was trained as a newspaper reporter, an investment services company insisted on seeing him once he returned stateside. And it was here that he both made his fortune and also met his crisis.

During the Depression, it became hard and nearly impossible to get money for anything at times, much less meet sales quotas. The general opinion was that times were hard. As V.P. in his company, over a group of sales people, he took his responsibility seriously. And was considering just quitting. But one night he had an epiphany. All the scenes he had experienced during his life which couldn't be explained suddenly were – in a bright flash of light. His life was changed. And he scoured his library for references to explain what he had found. His attitude changed into one of optimistic hope. And he started changing those of his sales staff.

With continuing research into this "mind-stuff" he found and tested various techniques with his salespeople. The results: doubled sales within a month. The next month after that, they doubled again. Soon his company was not only in the black, but was outselling all the similar companies in his city.

And soon, word spread of their success and he was invited to speak to other companies and their sales staff. And their sales also increased. With continued success, he was asked to write a brochure. That was successful and lead to a book. Soon he was doing nothing but lecturing and helping people with their lives through this "mind-stuff".

5. **J.B. Jones** – From a dirt-poor farm family, he was able to move consistently up to better conditions by his decisions and hard work. Once he had completed his service after World War II, he was attending college on the GI Bill while he spoke part time for the Napoleon Hill Foundation, on their philosophy of achievement. He studied related books and distilled that philosophy down to a simple four-step

formula that he knew would work. It became finally time for a test.

With two mortgages on his home, and a loan on his car, Jones borrowed another $10,000 to start a business out of his living room. Within four years, applying that formula, he was now worth 10's of millions and had a nationwide company with several other executives who themselves had become millionaires. Soon he also had a radio show, a TV show, and a bestseller book, all using his formula.

This became the start of Jim Rohn's career and several others. All from one test of a simple formula.

- - - -

All these authors, except Jones, are mentioned in Nightingale's recording. Jones' book was being written the same year Nightingale's Strangest Secret was recorded.

My tests in self-publishing public domain books lead me to this path of getting a course made for these books, since they all sell well and were related.

In fact, these books were used as the key support group for building the course and book you have in your hand. Reading and listening to these books over and over has given me clues and solutions for every problem I've run into.

But that is how I've changed my own beliefs, through months of repeated study.

And those studies lead me to you. The discovered ideas, written here and in those books, are all about what you can do with your own mind, your own beliefs.

All these secrets were found sitting in plain sight. These books are readily available on the Internet for download.

Yet people don't find them and won't read them. And that mystery is what still pulls us along. Anyone and everyone *can* be what they want to be and *can* have what they want to have.

Yet they *don't*.

We've covered some hints already about how and why this is.

There are more to come...

THE SECRET - SUCCESS AND FAILURE

When "The Secret" DVD came out, it had three fatal flaws:

> 1) It was too simple.

> 2) It was wildly popular.

> 3) It required belief to make it work.

It made a lot of money.

And it became a fad.

The reasons for its atmospheric rise and decline were a bit more complex, but not too much so:

- Our mainstream culture likes things complex.

- Our mainstream culture will "jump on the bandwagon" and then jump off again, because they are used to this.

- Our mainstream culture is trained to only believe in "science" and not faith-based anything.

Note that I prefaced everything with "mainstream."

In the U.S. this means the bi-coastal megalopolises, as well as the big cities (over 100,000 - including college towns which can surge well past that size seasonally.) When you have areas where the smaller towns butt right up against the big cities, they also adopt this attitude.

When you get (smaller) cities out by themselves, surrounded by vast acres of farm and ranch land, they can differ from this "mainstream" approach. (As a mass, this is known as "Flyover Country" - the land you see out your airplane window as you fly from coast to coast.)

Mainstream news and entertainment fits into this "big city" scenario.

This is coming up in our mystery sleuthing, in a couple of chapters after this, but I just wanted to let you know it's coming up.

This isn't something new. But there are historical examples.

Jesus had problems when he got to big city Jerusalem because the "mainstream culture" felt threatened. This is the nature of prophets and people being ahead of their time. Galileo had similar problems, as did Copernicus.

Complexity is welcome in megalopolises because it can be refuted or suborned by changing parts of it. Many parts = easily broken.

Ideas that run on faith are disliked because they can't be simply challenged or even outlawed easily.

Popular new ideas that take paying customers away from established money-making businesses and religions aren't appreciated. Hits them in their wallet.

The main point is that the Mainstreamers like the way things are and don't want things changed. So they become quite defensive about anything new and perceive it as a threat.

Again, we'll explore that shortly as to figure out the why.

Our point of including Byrne's *The Secret* as an illustration is to give you a preview of what you and I are up against as we keep on this approach.

It didn't matter that the Law of Attraction was first mentioned by name somewhere in the mid-to-late 1800's. Or that it was popular nationwide in the 1920's. Or that it is the basis of several natural laws which also affect our electric motors and even our smartphones.

It mattered that it was suddenly popular.

And so it was criticized.

Buckminster Fuller figured out the lags in technology adoption and figured out that it had to do with how soon things wore out. So new technology in buildings was resisted for between 50 and 100 years before architects and builders would adopt new designs. The one exception would be natural disasters, which could be a force to update building codes and new construction. But those disasters were only local, and so would only give examples of using these new approaches, not speed up overall acceptance.

Even today, the most efficient, lightest-weight, cheapest per square foot, and permanent building anyone can erect is Fuller's Geodesic dome. But it's still not widely adopted. It has never yet become mainstream.

This points to the mystery we're investigating in this book.

But it comes with a warning.

Try to tell people about what you learn in this book and you will probably find yourself widely criticized.

One reassuring note is that those same people criticize everything new that comes out. They also criticize everything that isn't "normal" (mainstream). Actually, you'll find them criticizing just about everything around them. (This also came up while digging around during research.)

So don't take it personally.

But do expect it to happen.

Yes, if you test what you find in *The Secret* DVD, you'll find that most of it does work right out of the package. Because it's based on natural principles and is simple. Anyone could understand and apply it and get results. Then, practice improves those results.

You actually don't have to believe it to test it for yourself.

Which brings up a warning. What I do tell you here, and will often repeat: *Don't accept anything I tell you except for testing*. Once you've tested it for yourself and proved it works for you, then and only then is it valid. *Only* where it's useful - to you.

The marketing for this book has been designed to be controversial.

Because, oddly, if people are critical of it, then it probably will get accepted more easily. Also, you can't get promoted through mainstream media unless you are controversial. Criticism and rejection are a big part of our culture.

BIG part.

So tell people about this in ways they'll easily understand.

But don't believe anything until you've tested it for yourself.

Once a product goes "mainstream" you'll see all sorts of people swearing it works, even though they have the package up on their living room shelf and it was never opened.

That's human nature. And that's what we're diving into next. (As well as what you can to do to succeed in a society like that.)

IS THIS "AS GOOD AS IT GETS?"

Jack Nicholson's character, in the movie of the same name, asks a waiting room full of other characters, "What if this is as good as it gets?"

Then he spends the rest of the movie disproving that question. But it sets the theme for the story.

It is our question, too.

The world we are told about in all our media is a strange, even bizarre, and violent world. Yet for the bulk of us (especially in the U.S.) it just isn't true. We don't see violence. We don't see starvation. People generally tend to live a rather safe and dull routine daily. (Some cities like Chicago are current exceptions.)

But can we do better?

Some of us have this itch to see what is on the other side of that mountain, who lives just beyond the horizon, how much of these problems we are given daily can be simply solved. A name for some of these are Adventurers, also called Entrepreneurs. These are the people who create the jobs so that the rest of us can live out our mundane existence in quiet safety and not too much discomfort.

And those jobs allow us to buy our food and clothes and cars, as well as paying for our movies and entertainment. Sure, we have to work 40-hour weeks (more or less, depending on regulations) but we have a way to earn the income we need to provide for our families and even take some vacations now and then.

But can we do better?

The masses who live and work in Mundania seem content enough with their jobs and wages and movies and dining out. And everywhere they go, they deal with people who have jobs and wages and movies and dining out.

They simply don't know what they are missing. The possibilities for each of us is endless. The abilities we can regain, and skills and talent are limitless.

We can each have and be anything and everything we ever dreamed of.

Instead of working 40 years for someone else at a job you weren't particularly fond of, only to retire on a limited income and dependent on government checks to round things out – you could instead work only at things you loved to do. You could be paid so much that you feel obligated to give most of it away, because you couldn't think of anything useful to do with it.

Shooting for the starts in order to hit the moon would be a daily occurrence in your life. You could live constantly at your peak performance levels and love every second of life.

But we don't.

We could, though.

The only limits are our own mindset and how we've stacked it.

Surely, it couldn't be that simple...

POSTSCRIPT

Now that you've seen what passes for the "real' world, it's time to look behind the curtain to find the actual world and who's been running it.

Surprises await...

PREVIEW OF PART 2

There's a new world ahead of you. This book you just finished does nothing except invite you to this new adventure.

The actual world is different that what you've been led to believe all this time, what you used to consider as "real."

You've been introduced to the main characters in this story.

But these are only helpers. It's *your* story that we are interested in. *You* are the hero(ine) here.

Whether you choose to continue on is up to you.

And if you test and believe what you've been told up to this point, in this book or outside of it, your life will change forever. That's guaranteed.

The next three parts to this book should help make that transition easier. Not smoother, just simpler.

Because you've gotten where you are by what you've believed up to this point, and what you've used to accomplish and achieve and acquire up to now.

Beyond that is a future that you will create based on what you believe from this point forward.

The point that "as you believe, you succeed" isn't a new idea. Sure, Napoleon Hill had his version, and it's been repeated time and again. But an earlier version of that statement was recently traced back to Socrates. The roots of it go to prehistory and our verbal traditions.

So you could say that it's withstood the tests of time.

That doesn't matter as much as if it survives your own tests.

It's what you believe that counts. Not me, not any other book or teacher or mentor you've had. Just you and your beliefs count.

What You Can Expect Coming Up...

- Why you have gotten scammed in the past and how to stop this happening from now on.

- The single source of all our failures.

- Why success can come to anyone, but exceptional success comes *only* to a small percentage every generation.

- How the groups you belong to can keep you from your success.

- The reason that the cause of your failures can also cause you to succeed.

- Why scientists get it so wrong so often.

- Are thoughts truly contagious? Can we "catch" a bad habit like the flu?

- If you do learn these success tips, will you wind up super successful or a super failure? (And how to choose your fate...)

APPENDIX

LINKS FOR PART 1

How Science gets it half wrong every time:

- PLOS article:
  http://journals.plos.org/plosmedicine/article?id=10.1371/journal.pmed.0020124

- Readable version in The Guardian
  https://www.theguardian.com/science/occams-corner/2013/sep/17/scientific-studies-wrong

- or The Economist
  http://www.economist.com/news/leaders/21588069-scientific-research-has-changed-world-now-it-needs-change-itself-how-science-goes-wrong

How Science fudges its processes – Rupert Sheldrake:

- Rupert Sheldrake on wikipedia -
  https://en.wikipedia.org/wiki/Rupert_Sheldrake

- His banned TED talk -
  https://steemit.com/science/@morpheustitania/the-science-delusion-banned-ted-talk - fortunately that page also has a partial transcript.

Surveys of government trust by their people:

- http://www.people-press.org/2015/11/23/1-trust-in-government-1958-2015/

- http://www.gallup.com/poll/5392/trust-government.aspx

Reports that media isn't trusted:

- http://bigstory.ap.org/article/35c595900e0a4ffd99f bdc48a336a6d8/poll-vast-majority-americans-dont-trust-news-media and

- Gallup http://www.gallup.com/poll/185927/americans-trust-media-remains-historical-low.aspx

Thomas Kuhn's Paradigm Shift

https://en.wikipedia.org/wiki/Paradigm_shift

BIBLIOGRAPHY

You can find many of these books and materials available and reviewed on http://livesensical.com/myga-books

Brande, Dorothea

Wake Up and Live!

Becoming a Writer

Bristol, Claude M.

The Magic of Believing

Byrne, Rhonda

The Secret (DVD)

Campbell, Joseph

Hero With a Thousand Faces

Carson, Rachel

Silent Spring

Cialdini, Robert

Influence

Coyne, Shawn

Story Grid

Ehrlich, Paul

Population Bomb

Gladwell, Malcolm

Outliers

Blink

Hill, Napoleon

Think and Grow Rich

Master Key to Riches

10 Lessons in Cosmic Habitforce

James, William

The Principles of Psychology

The Will to Believe

Jones, James Breckenridge

If You Can Count to Four

King, Dr. Serge Kahili

The Seven Principles of Huna (lecture)

King, Stephen

On Writing

Long, Max Freedom

Introduction to Huna

Huna: Recovering the Ancient Magic

Maslow, Abraham

A Theory of Human Motivation

Nightingale, Earl

The Strangest Secret (transcript)

How to Completely Change Your Life in 30 Seconds

Ponder, Catherine

The Dynamic Laws of Prosperity

Schwartz, Eugene

Breakthrough Advertising

Breakthrough Copywriter (based on his talks)

Vogler, Chris

> *The Writer's Journey*

Whitely, Opal

> *The Journal of an Understanding Heart*

Worstell, Robert C

> *Go Thunk Yourself*
>
> *Go Thunk Yourself, Again*
>
> *What Jesus Really Said*

The **Living Sensical Manifesto** *may be downloaded at no cost (or even opt-in) at:* https://calm.li/LSmanifesto

NOTES:

Part 1 Notes

The core idea this book has been built around is to get you to observe, think, and act for yourself. To not depend on others opinions, observations, and conclusions to stack your own mindset from.

Where there is controversy in this book, it is blatently there to get you to do just that.

By survey, people don't trust the government or broadcast media. They've tended to trust scientists, but this is starting to dissolve, especially where scientists have been exposed as massaging their data in order to get results. (All apparently in order to agree with their funding sources.)

I've only given you some short links to find out about these. Practically, each area can be the subject of long papers and even books. If you go to research these, I'm sure you'll find many on both sides of this argument.

The core scene has to do with whether the individual is able to think on their own, or whether it's more efficient and profitable to rely on central sources of information.

When you dig into these studies, you'll see that as our communications and content technologies improve, we have become less reliant on centralized sources of data. During World War II, central control of our TV programming was possible. With our smartphones and Internet, it's highly difficult (though China and other countries are still trying.)

People don't like to give up their choice. It's one of the few abilities which are so hard-wired that it can't be taken away by anyone. "Brainwashing" is temporary at best. Some psychiatrists say that it takes about 12 years to fully undo the cult programming once a person leaves their influence.

And there is the cultural backlash, as we'll see in Part 2, where I discuss the "Bucket Crab" phenomenon. That backlash is probably why the phenomenon of Freedom known in the United States is taking so long to be adopted in other countries. While Russia has a democcratic state in name, Putin is still an example of the old regime being supported. As this goes to press, his surveyed support is higher in Russia than Obama's ever was in the U.S.

The key to this book is that it is just an introduction to a much wider subject of how to (re)stack your mindset. So the main idea is to start discussions, to bring up the ideas touched on and develop awareness.

There is no attempt to get people to think the same way or have the same belief systems. Quite the contrary. We are each individuals and that is what gives our world true diversity, not sex or skin color or cultural background.

Most of these authors mentioned have been pooh-poohed by our culture and disregarded as "old." The principles discussed are timeless and have been mentioned and popular in every decade of recorded history.

It used to be a tradition to revere the old. Perhaps that is a great tradition to revive.

ACKNOWLEDGMENTS

Many thanks to Ed Grunzel, Simone Agarrat, RT, Sarah M, and Vasant Alfred for helping me get this book ready. You are appreciated more than you know.

INDEX

BONUS 2

I'd like to give you a few more things to help you out:

> 0) *A Cheat Sheet for Part 1*, where you get a list of the key datums covered, all in a simple PDF. This is so you can test the data you've read for yourself.

> 1) *Access to a member's only library* of references which give the background and more tools to enable you improve your own success chances.

> 2) *An upcoming course* that can assist you in changing your mental habits and get failure -free if you want. (No charge to subscribers.)

> 3) *A personal line to the author* for any assistance you want in learning to apply this book.

> 4) *...And advanced offers plus discounts* for the rest of the books in this series, as well as other versions such as audio and even video versions.

All you have to do is to sign up using the link below.

Do this now. Click or type this into your browser for instant access:

http://livesensical.com/mygajoin/